The TWENTY THIRD INDIAN DIVISION

BURMA   MALAYA   JAVA

The Naval & Military Press Ltd

Published by

The Naval & Military Press Ltd
Unit 5 Riverside, Brambleside
Bellbrook Industrial Estate
Uckfield, East Sussex
TN22 1QQ England

Tel: +44 (0)1825 749494

www.naval-military-press.com

In reprinting in facsimile from the original, any imperfections are inevitably reproduced and the quality may fall short of modern type and cartographic standards.

23rd INDIAN DIVISION AS IN JUNE 1942
Formations/Units and Commanders

Div. Comd.	Maj. Gen.	R.A. SAVORY, C.B., D.S.O., M.C.
C. R. A.	Brigadier	R. W. ANDREWS, O.B.E., M.C.
C. I.	Lt. Col.	R. A. N. WIMBERLEY
A/Q	Lt. Col.	M. P. B. REEVES
C.R.E.	Lt. Col.	R. S. T. C. DAVIDSON
Comd. *1 Bde*	Brigadier	F. V. R. WOODHOUSE
CO 1 SEAFORTH	Lt. Col.	W. MacFARLANE
CO 1 PATIALA	Lt. Col.	BALWANT SINGH SIDU BAHADUR, C.B.E., D.S.O., O.B.I.
CO 1 Assam Regt.	Lt. Col.	BROWN, O.B.E.
Comd. *37 Bde*	Brigadier	H. V. L. H. COLLINGRIDGE, O.B.E.
CO 3/3 G. R.	Lt. Col.	FOSTER, M.C.
CO 3/5 R.G.R.	Lt. Col.	J. F. MARINDIN
CO 3/10 G.R.	Lt. Col.	R.B.E. UPTON
Comd. *49 Bde*	Brigadier	THOMAS
CO 4/5 MAHRATTA L.I.	Lt. Col.	R. L. ISAACS
CO 2/19 HYBAD	Lt. Col.	A. W. S. MALLABY, C.I.E., O.B.E.
CO 5/6 RAJ RIF	Lt. Col.	R. D. AMBROSE, O.B.E., M.C.
1st IND FIELD REGT.	Lt. Col.	L. S. GALLACHER
158 FIELD REGT.	Lt. Col.	GALLOWAY

INDO-BURMA BORDER – BURMA

The TWENTY-THIRD INDIAN DIVISION

Designed by Maj.-Gen. (now Lt. Gen.) Savory, the 23rd Indian Division flash was intended to be symbolic and equally intelligible to both B.O.R. and I.O.R. without being offensive to the Hindu or Muslim. It was also intended to be capable of a slightly bawdy interpretation. Gen. Savory says that frequently he had to insist that the result was "a fighting cock, not a b---y rooster".

An illustrated story telling of the Division's exploits and achievements from 1942 until 1945.

MALAYA and JAVA

DIVISIONAL COMMANDERS

Major-General (now Lt. Gen.) R.A. SAVORY, C.B., D.S O., M.C., as commander of the 11th Indian Infantry Brigade fought against the Italians and Germans in the Middle East campaigns of 1940 and 1941.

In January, 1942, he became commander of the 23rd Indian Division, then on the vital Indo-Burma border, and remained with it until June 1943. He was subsequently Director of Infantry, and Commander Persia & Iraq Command. He is now Adjutant General in India, and the first Colonel of the Sikh Light Infantry.

✠ ✠ ✠

Major-General (now Lt. Gen.) O. L. ROBERTS, C.B.E., D.S.O., commanded the 20th Indian Infantry Brigade in 1941 and the 16th British Infantry Brigade in 1942. He saw fighting in all the main theatres of war, except France.

He took over command of the 23rd Indian Division in August 1943, and successfully led it through some of the toughest fighting of the Burma campaign.

In 1945, he was promoted to the rank of Lt. Gen. to command 34 Indian Corps, and has since been appointed D.A.G. at the War Office.

✠ ✠ ✠

Major-General D. C. HAWTHORN, C.B., D.S.O. rose from the appointment of G. S O. 2 in 7th Indian Division to command 62 Brigade of 19th Indian Division. In April 1945 he succeeded to the command of 23rd Indian Division. Since then he has brought it with great success through Malaya and Java under the most difficult and trying circumstances.

✠ ✠ ✠

*

Major Gen.
(now Lt. Gen.)
R.A. SAVORY,
C.B., D.S.O., M. C.

*

Major-Gen. (now Lt. Gen.) O. L. ROBERTS C.B.E., D.S.O.

Major-Gen. D. C. HAWTHORN, C. B., D. S. O.

SOME "BAHADURS" OF THE DIVISION

✢ ✢ ✢

MAJOR (now Lt. Col.) W. M. MACKAY, D.S.O., M. C., 4/5th Mahratta Light Infantry was awarded the M. C. for gallantry when commanding a company at Okkan in 1943; and also the D.S.O. in 1943 when his C.O. having been killed, he extricated his battalion from a very difficult situation during the battle of Saibong.

✢ ✢ ✢

MAJOR J. W. ARKELL, M. C. and Bar, 3/5th Royal Gurkha Rifles, won his first M. C. for gallantry when his patrol successfully ambushed several Japanese in 1943. His Bar was won when leading two companies of his Battalion against an enemy position at Milestone 93 on the Assam-Burma front.

✢ ✢ ✢

CAPTAIN L. THOMPSON, M.C., H.Q., 23rd Indian Division Transport Section received the M.C. for gallantry on 9th Dec. '45 when, as M.T. commander of 200 vehicles proceeding from Batavia to Bandoeng, he encountered three road blocks with heavy opposition. Casualties were sustained, and Capt. Thompson, although wounded engaged the enemy, and brought the convoy to its destination.

✢ ✢ ✢

HAVILDAR YESHWANT MANE, I.D.S. M., 6/5th Mahratta Light Infantry, was awarded the decoration for exceptional courage and leadership during the period May to August 1944 in Burma.

✢ ✢ ✢

LANCE NAIK CHIMAJI MORE, I.D.S.M., 6/5th Mahratta Light Infantry, received his decoration for bravery and initiative which saved a whole company from sustaining severe casualties at Sourabaya on 30th October, 1945.

✢ ✢ ✢

C. Q. M. H. BAJAJIRAO SHINDE, M.M., 6/5th Mahratta Light Infantry, received his decoration for outstanding courage and initiative in action at Sourabaya on 28th October, 1945.

✢ ✢ ✢

LANCE HAVILDAR DULBAHADUR GHALE, M. M., 3/3rd Gurkha Rifles, received his award for distinguished services and gallantry on the Tiddim Road on 21st May, 1944.

✢ ✢ ✢

SEPOY BABURAO POWAR, M. M., 6/5th Mahratta Light Infantry, received his decoration for undertaking an extremely dangerous mission which might well have been suicidal, on 29th October, 1945, at Sourabaya.

✢ ✢ ✢

Brig. Balwant Singh Sidu Bahadur, C.B.E., O.B.I., O.C., 1 Patialas, receives the D.S.O. from the Commander-in-Chief in India, Field Marshal Sir Claude Auchinleck, during the latter's visit to the Division.

Sub. Akbar Ali, M. C., 1/16 Punjab. Decorated for gallantry at Imphal, April '44.

Jem. Achhar Singh, M.C., 1/16 Punjab. Silenced enemy M.G. at Imphal, May '44.

Jem. Arjan Singh, I.D.S.M., 1/16 Punjab. Captured enemy position at Imphal, May '44.

Hav. Shah Wali, I.D.S.M., 1/16 Punjab. Great courage in attack at Imphal, July '44.

Hav. Kala Khan, M. M., 1/16 Punjab. Captured enemy post at Imphal in July '44.

Hav. Gurdas Ram, I. D. S.M., 1/16 Punjab. Decorated for gallantry at Imphal, May ,'44.

Nk. Mohd. Yakub, I. D. S.M., 1/16 Punjab,. Forced enemy to withdraw at Imphal, July '44

Sub. Tek Chand, M. C., 123 Ind. Coy. R.I.A S.C. Saved many lives in Java Oct, '45.

Hav. Ganesh Naik, I. D. S.M., 6/5 M.L.I. Decorated for devoted service, May—Aug. '44.

Nk. M. Aroki Swami, M.I.D., 323 Ind. Fd. Pk. Coy. R.I.E. Gallant service, Nov. '43—May '44.

Sub. Mansab Khan, M.I.D., Pr. Unit C.M.P. (D. Distinguished service, Burma—Assam '43—'44.

Nk. Mohd. Ghani, M.I.D., and Nk Subbarayan, M.I.D., 3 Ind. Fd. Regt. R.I.A. Both mentioned in recognition of distinguished services on the Assam—Burma front.

R.H.M. C.P. Kumaran, M.M., Nk. D. George, M.I.D., and Hav. Krishna Kotty, M.I.D., 3 Ind. Fd. Regt. R.I.A. R.H.M. Kumaran was decorated for gallantry in Java, Nk. George and Hav. Kutty were mentioned for gallant services in Java and Burma.

Sub. Appa Rao, M.I.D., 323 Ind. Fd. Pk. Coy. R.I.E. Gallant service in Manipur campaign.

Sweeper Wazir, M.M., 5/6 Raj. Rif. Courage and disregard of own safety in Java.

Maj. G. E. Dubois, M.C., 5/6 Raj. Rif. Fearlessness during enemy attack at Shenam.

Sub. Farman Ali, M.B.E., 5/6 Raj. Rif. Great devotion to duty during training.

Jem. Kaluram, M.C., 5/6 Raj. Rif. Fearlessness in leading bayonet charge in Burma.

Nk. Mohd. Khan, M.M. and Bar, 5/6 Raj. Rif. Bravery at Shenam and Java.

Hav. Leku Ram, B.E.M., 5/6 Raj. Rif. Loyalty and devotion to duty of a high order.

Hav. C. Nagaish, M.I.D., Hav. S. Sudamani Pillai, M.I.D., and Nk. N. Appu Shetty, M.I.D., of 23 Ind. Div. Sigs. All three mentioned for gallant and distinguished services in Burma from Nov.-'43 — May. '44.

Maj. P.S. Thappa, M.C., 4/5 M.L.I. Bravery and leadership at Imphal July '44.

Sub-Maj. Sadu Jagdale, M.C., 4/5 M.L.I. For gallantry in action; Imphal area, July '44.

L/Nk. Narayan Shinde, I.D.S.M., Hav. Sambhaji Bhuingde, I.D.S.M., Nk. Pursuram Kadam, M.M. L/Nk. Shinde won I.D.S.M. at Imphal in June '44, Hav. Bhuingde at Ukhrul in '44, and Nk. Kadam for extreme gallantry at Sourabaya, Oct. '45.

Capt. R.M Rice, M.I.D., 2 Ind. A. Tk. Regt., R.I.A. Distinguished service at Langgol.

Jem. Mansabdar Khan, M.I.D. and Jem. Raj Wali, M.I.D., 2 Ind. A. Tk. Regt., R.I.A. Both won recognition for gallant and distinguished services in the Imphal area during '44 and also at Langgol in June '44.

Q.M.H. Ghulam Mohd., M.I.D., and L/Nk Mohd. Zaman, M.I.D., 2 Ind. A.Tk. Regt. R.I.A. Both were mentioned in recognition of their exemplary conduct in the Tiddim road area during April—May, '44.

Sgt. J.W. Frankish, M.M., R.A.F. (attached Force 136). Bravery in Java, Nov., '45.

Maj. A. C. Meikle, M. C., 3/10 G. R. Decorated for bravery on Scraggy Hill, '44.

Jem. Dal Bahadur Limbu, I.O.M., 3/10 G. R. Decorated for bravery. Chindwin, May '43.

Maj. H. C. Pulley, M.C., 3/3 G. R. Decorated for bravery during the campaign.

Hav. Kharak Bahadur Rai, M.I.D., and Hav. Padam Bahadur Gurung, M. M., both 3/10 G. R. Hav. Rai mentioned for bravery at Magelang, Java in Oct., '45, and Hav. Gurung decorated for gallantry at M.S. 98, March, '44.

Nk. Ajirat Rai, I. D. S. M., and Nk. Mehal Sing Rai M. M. and Bar both 3/10 G. R. The former won I. D. S. M. for bravery at Scraggy Hill, and the latter the M. M. for gallantry at Shenam and Phalbung.

Nk. Ramchandra Bahadur Ghale, I.D.S.M., 3/3 G.R. Great bravery in Assam and Burma.

L/Nk. Dande Gurung, M.M., L/Hav. Panthabir Thapa M.M., and Sep. Sunapainkhi Gurung, M.M. L/Nk. Gurung was decorated for bravery at Cyprus Hill, and L/Hav. Thapa at Malta Hill. Sep. Gurung won his award for gallantry at Imphal.

Sub. Durgabahadur Thapa, M.C., 3/3 G.R. Decorated in recognition of distinguished services at Sanakeital near Ukhrul, 27th April '44.

Brig. N. MacDonald, D.S.O., as commander 4/5, R.G.R. was awarded immediate D.S.O. Appointed commander 37 Ind. Inf. Bde. in July '44.

HONOURS AND AWARDS

The following figures give the total number of immediate and periodic awards:—

	Immediate	Periodic	Total
D.S.O.	2	12	14
Bar to D.S.O.	. .	1	1
2nd Bar to D.S.O.	. .	1	1
M.C.	27	72	99
Bar to M.C.	4	40	44
D.C.M.	1	4	5
M.M.	65	61	126
Bar to M.M.	1	4	5
I.O.M.	7	2	9
I.D.S.M.	31	25	56
Bar to I.D.S.M.	1	. .	1
Mentioned in Despatches	. .	562	562
Certificates of Gallantry	31	17	48
C.B.	. .	1	1
C.B.E.	. .	1	1
O.B.E.	. .	8	8
M.B.E.	. .	21	21
B.E.M.	. .	2	2
M.S.M.	. .	4	4
C.I.E.	. .	1	1
Commendation Cards	. .	4	4
	170	843	1,013

2. These awards are for Gallant and Distinguished Service with 23 Ind. Div. in BURMA, NORTH-EAST FRONTIER, INDIA, MALAYA and JAVA.

They cover the period from the first operation by the Div. in June 1942 to the end of 1945. Recommendations for further awards for service in JAVA have been submitted through higher authority but have not yet been approved. (Dated July 1946).

GENERAL MAP OF BURMA

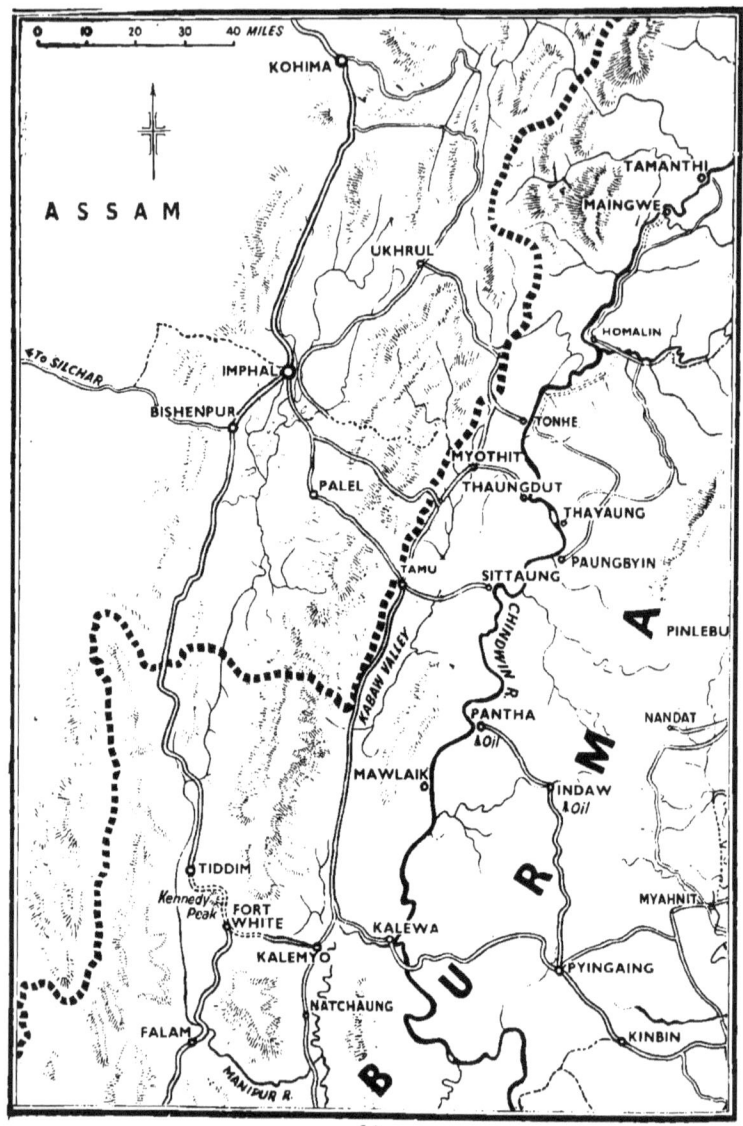

THE TWENTY-THIRD
INDIAN DIVISION

The 1942 Campaign

THE 23RD INDIAN DIVISION first went into action on the borders of Burma and Assam. Men from Nepal, India, Bombay, Hyderabad, Assam and the British Isles combined to create a new fighting formation of the Indian Army, ready to throw back the Japanese invader.

In June, 1942, the first patrolling started from Imphal. Throughout the monsoon until November the Division formed defensive positions and covered the withdrawal of General Alexander's Army. Over a long and difficult supply route, rations were often short. In June, while the Division was settling in the Imphal area, its transport was clearing Burma refugees back to Dimapur in India.

Long distance patrols went out day after day, seeking out the enemy and getting to know the jungle; in November, 1942, the road from Palel to Tamu was reopened by the Divisional Engineers, who in two months had improved the surface sufficiently for the entire Division to be concentrated and maintained in the Kabaw valley. Again patrolling started North, South

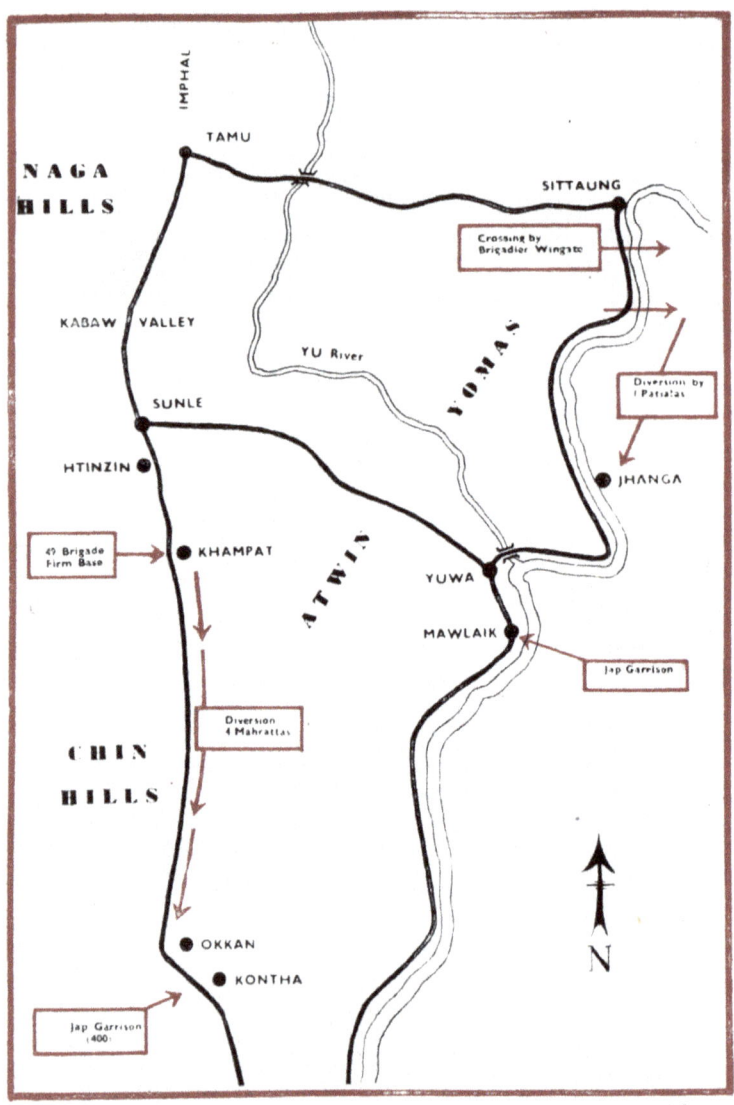

DIVERSION OF 4TH MAHARATTA LIGHT INFANTRY, 16th February, 1943. This illustrates the diversion made by the Battalion to cover Brigadier Wingate's crossing of the Chindwin.

and East from Tamu; as far as the Chindwin the men of the Division operated.

In India Brigadier Wingate had started to train his first force to penetrate and attack behind the Japanese lines. When Wingate's band set out, men from 23rd Indian Division escorted them 20 miles beyond the Chindwin. As a diversion 4 Mahratta Light Infantry were selected from 49 Brigade and from the position manned by 6 Mahratta Light Infantry made an attack on Okkan, near Kalemyo, after a swift advance down Kabaw valley. In this expedition they got the first Japanese proved killed by the Division and L/Naik Maruti Shindi was awarded the I.D.S.M. Later, when Wingate returned, his men barely able to stand, 23rd Indian Division covered their retreat. Two bridgeheads were

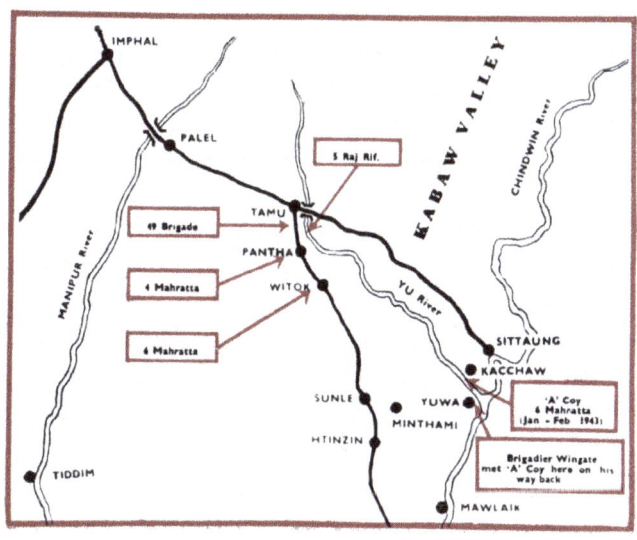

SITUATION OF 49 BRIGADE IN THE SPRING OF 1943.
Manipur and Burma. This diagram shows 49 Brigade's positions.

made on the Jap side of the Chindwin, the first was formed by the 1st Patiala Infantry, later relieved by 3/5 R.G.R. and the second by the 1st Bn. Seaforth, commanded by Lt. Col. W. Macfarlane, later by 3/10 G.R. Sgt. (now CSM) J.O. O'Neill of the Seaforths, in command of two sections on 20th April, 1943, met a Jap company. They withdrew to the bank of the Chindwin and while his men swam across he covered their withdrawal. Twenty enemy were killed in this action for which Sgt. O'Neill received the D.C.M.

Constant patrolling by the battalions, and sudden small attacks in the jungle, distracted the enemy's attention from Wingate's exhausted men. With the approach of the '43 monsoon the Palel-Tamu fair weather road was again closed. Another enemy in the valley was malaria and, at this time, Mepacrine and other preventive measures still had to become general issue. In November, 1943, the 23rd had been holding its sector of the Assam frontier—over 100 miles long—for more than 18 months. Difficulties in climate, disease and supply had been met and overcome. Though the health of the troops was not good, morale was always high. Then, as new troops arrived from India, the majority of the Division was withdrawn for four months rest and training in the healthier winter climate of the Imphal plain. General Savory left the Division and General Roberts took over the command.

When withdrawing, news came from the Chin Hills to the South that the 17th Division was being heavily pressed. The 16th Punjab Regt., with a battery of 28 Mountain Regt., went to the assistance of 63 Brigade. The fighting partnership between the two divisions, "The Black Cat" and "The Fighting Cock" had begun.

The Punjabis were surrounded, but, fighting hard, they withdrew in a night action after killing many enemy. They had suffered severely, losing their C.O., Lt.-Col. S. D. Willcock, M. C., the Adjutant, Q M., and two other officers with 70 I.O.Rs.

*   *   *

Rest and Preparation.

DURING THE REST the Division got valuable training, including work with tanks, while reinforcements joined from India. Soon 23rd Division were again ready for action. Army HQ Intelligence reports showed that a big Japanese offensive was about to be launched on Imphal. But now the time of taking the enemy's attacks was coming to a close. Although an enemy offensive was near, the 14th Army was making plans for his defeat. General Wingate was to lead a second attack, this time an air-borne landing in Northern Burma on a larger scale than anything before.

Again 23rd Division was given the task of making a diversion. 1 Ind. Inf. Bde. and 3/3 G.R. under command of Lt. Col. D'Arcy-McCarthy, M.C., were given the task of crossing the Chindwin at approximately the same places where Wingate had crossed the year before. They moved to Sittaung and started a deception scheme. The Q.M. was dressed as a Brigadier and "inspected" various units. This was seen by the Japs.

First steps were now taken for the Jap attack—their last attempt to invade India. The 50th Indian Parachute Brigade arrived in Imphal and came under command of the Division, relieving 49 Brigade of the job of guarding the approach through the Naga Hills to the North of Imphal. Supply lines were shortened. 17th and 20th Divisions were withdrawn from the Kabaw valley nearer their base in Imphal.

The newly-formed 14th Army was on the eve of its first battle. General Slim, the Commander, decided *"that for the first time we should fight the Japanese when the precarious line of communication was behind them and not behind us."* When the attack came, 23rd Division was centred on the Imphal plain, and had to cover the Tiddim road some distance South of Imphal. General Roberts was ordered to provide an attack force at Ukhrul for a counter-attack against the Japanese crossing the Chindwin.

✤ ✤ ✤

Start of Imphal Battle.

WORK OF BRIGADES

THE ENEMY'S FIRST MOVE in early March, 1944 was a wide encircling movement through the Chin Hills, threatening to cut 17th Division's supply lines. Time was vital. To meet the threat 37 Brigade was moved late on March 14th to milestone 38 on the road South from Imphal into the Chin Hills. The 3/5 R.G.R. from the Brigade were pushed ahead to help the isolated detachments of 17th Division already hard pressed. The 3/3 G. R. had, after covering 100 miles from Sittaung in 24 hours, joined 37 Brigade. Then, when forward troops of 37 Brigade were themselves cut off by the enemy, the whole Division less one Brigade started fighting from Imphal to meet 17th Division. Brigadier Esse, commanding 49 Brigade, was sent forward to establish a secure base, "admin box" and keep the road open, while 37 Brigade and 17th Division forced their way towards each other.

There followed one of the bloodiest fights in the campaign. The scene was the muddy, winding Tiddim road with jungle-clad slopes rising steeply on either side. In the background were ranges of mountains covered in almost impenetrable jungle. The enemy, from the elite 33rd Jap Division, were infiltrated by battalions up to the road where they split the Brigade. Three attempts were necessary before by joint efforts the 3/3 had met the two battalions ahead, 3/5 and 3/10. The wounded had no resting place, being put side by side on the road itself, and by the time the two advance battalions had been relieved over 250 casualties had accumulated.

When they met 17th Division finally, 37 Brigade was given the task of covering the withdrawal of 17th Division to Imphal. 49 Brigade were ordered to fall back to

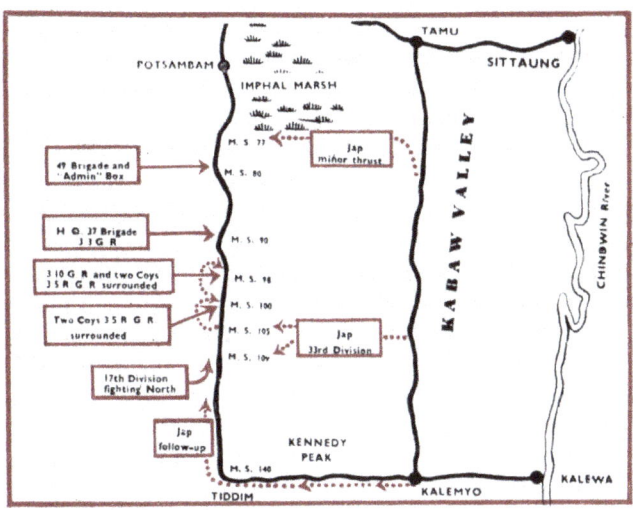

TIDDIM ROAD BATTLE. March 1944. 'The scene was the muddy winding Tiddim Road ..' This shows how the Japanese split 37 Brigade trying to link with 17th Division.

another defensive position near Imphal. Eventually, on the night of April 9th, 37 Brigade withdrew through 49 Brigade into the Imphal plain. They had been marching and fighting without a rest since March 15th. Patrolling further East, 1 Brigade had carried out the Chindwin diversions, but their activities did not worry the Japanese very much, who had already firmly fixed their attack on the Imphal front and were not aware of the menace from Wingate's expedition.

When the size of the Japanese attack became apparent, 1 Brigade was ordered to return to the Imphal plain without waiting for the return of their patrols out on the far side of the Chindwin, who eventually got back with only three casualties. As the Brigade moved the enemy started the attack in strength northwards up the Kabaw valley.

In another sector of the defence the 50th Indian Parachute Brigade, led by Lt.-Col. J. B. Hope-Campbell (with the 4th Battalion Mahratta Light Infantry attached from 49 Brigade) had been meeting since 22nd March a Japanese offensive through the Naga Hills with the object of capturing Imphal and the airfield. The parachutists had only arrived a few days previously and now found themselves completely cut off at Sangshak and forced to fight a delaying action for several days, in which the 4th Mahrattas, commanded by Lt.-Col. J. N. Trim, played a leading part. 71 Field Company, 582 Field Battery, R.A. and 15 Mountain Battery, also played a gallant part. Although about a thousand of the enemy were killed and wounded, attempts in air supply failed and—with no troops available to relieve it—the Brigade was ordered to fight its way out. But the first part of the battle had been completed successfully.

The job of defeating the enemy had started and General Slim wrote later: *"The enemy, by constantly attacking and reinforcing failure, fell into our hands and it was at this period, especially round Imphal, that the process of wearing him out began."*

*   *   *

SANGSHAK — March 1944

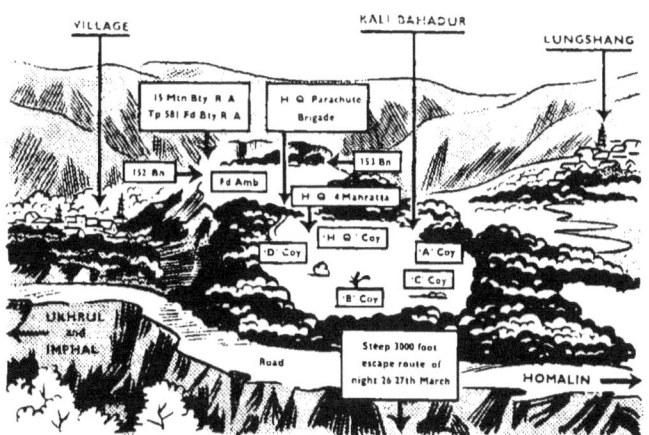

Imphal Cut Off

23rd DIVISION ATTACK THE
15th JAP DIVISION

4TH CORPS, in which 23rd Division served, was reinforced by 5th Division, who had made a lightning move from the Arakan front. Now, as anticipated, the Japanese cut the road from the railhead to Imphal and deployed for the attack on Kohima. This meant troops on the Imphal plain becoming entirely dependent on air transport for ammunition, petrol and supplies. Casualties were evacuated by Dakotas.

For the defence of Imphal town 23rd Division were given the job of covering the approach from the North-East ; 5th Division had to hold the North. The task was to be carried out in the spirit of the 14th Army—offensively—by an attack on the 15th Japanese Division, when it was hoped to capture Lt.-Gen. Yamuchi. His headquarters was known to be on the Ukhrul road running North-East from Imphal into the Naga Hills.

General Roberts drew up the plans. 37 Brigade was to make a frontal attack along the road while 1 Brigade on 11th April carried out an encircling movement by a secret cross-country march through the hills to the East. 49 Brigade went into Corps reserve but was given the job of clearing some enemy resistance in the hills west of the road.

The operation started. In two actions 37 Brigade killed many of the enemy. After a march over mountain tracks scarcely passable to mules, 1 Brigade found the Jap H.Q. The Seaforths captured much equipment and documents.

The personnel of the H.Q. had moved and the enemy started counter-attacks, which were beaten off. He was then cleared from the hills dominating the area. The only supply road to 1 Brigade was a mule track along which it had advanced and decision was made to reopen the road so that casualties could be taken to hospital before further operations. These, which had already been planned, involved an advance over hill country even worse than that already crossed. The hills were large, jungle-clad and precipitous, being ideal for defence and giving little opportunity to the attacker. 37 Brigade and 1 Brigade working to each other, finally opened the road on 22nd April and a jeep convoy came through, bringing back all the casualties.

*   *   *

Battle of Lam-mu

THE ENEMY HEADQUARTERS now was a village, Lam-mu, a few miles West of the road. Under cover of an attack northwards by 1st. Seaforth, during which CQMS Stevens won the D.C.M., 1 Brigade, moving by mountain tracks, surprised the enemy in their new headquarters. The attacking company smashed into the administrative area, killing many enemy, but unfortunately again missed the Commander, now known to the Division as "The Rat". He escaped into the jungle.

From 37 Brigade the 3/3 G.R. were sent to the West to cut off the escape route, but the country was too difficult and the enemy, although they left many dead behind, were able to escape to the North. Meanwhile 49 Brigade had, after severe fighting, mopped up the Japanese pockets of resistance.

The Division was ready to continue the fight.

Relief of 20th Division

BATTLE OF SHENAM

ON MAY 18TH, 23rd Division relieved 20th Division at Shenam. This was a complicated operation as troops of 20th Division were close to the Japanese and the only road was in full view of the enemy. However, with careful staff work, the changeover was successful.

While the enemy was being caught and smashed by 5th, 20th and 17th Divisions, the new task for 23rd Division was to hold back the enemy task force South of Palel, which contained his main armour and artillery strength.

The Japanese continued to throw more and more troops into the battle. 23rd Division had to prevent an enemy advance on Palel airfield. 37 Brigade under Brig. H.V. Collinridge and later Brig. J. Marindin, D.S.O., was in possession here with 1st Seaforth and the 5th Rajputana Rifles under command. For the rest of May, June and well into July the enemy continually shelled and there was hardly a day on which an attack was not made, the enemy trying to cut communications and prevent the Palel airfield being used. Every single battalion of the Division was involved in heavy and successful fighting on the hills, around. As the monsoon approached living conditions got steadily worse and units were, in many cases living in continual mist with intermittent heavy

THE PALEL AIRFIELD, scene of bitter fighting. A Dakota aircraft wings its way over the field preparatory to landing with much-needed supplies.

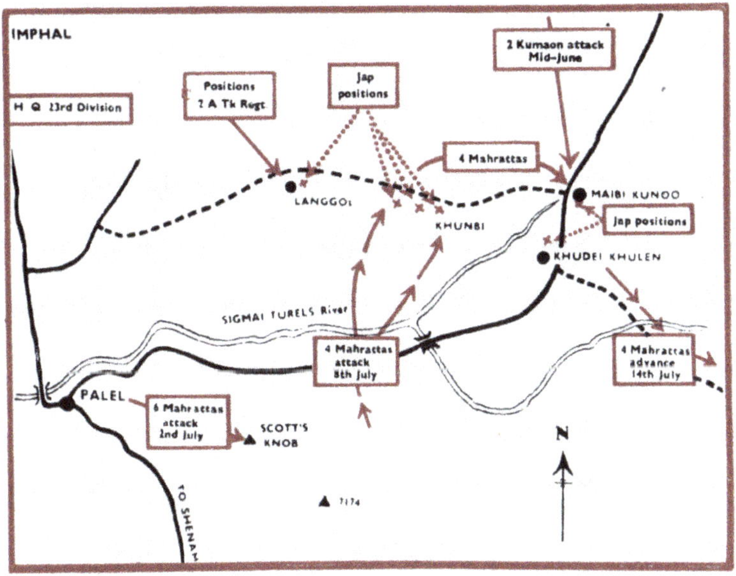

OPERATIONS OF 49 BRIGADE, July 1944. Shows how the Brigade cleared Japanese infiltration from plain behind Shenam position on Palel airfield.

R.A.F. AID GURKHAS AGAINST JAP HELD FEATURE.
A Gurkha attack on a hill in the PALEL sector was preceded by valuable R.A.F. and R.I.A.F. support. Gurkhas in action during the attack.

rain. Visibility was only up to 100 yards and they had very little cover and were never dry. The more exposed battalion positions on Scraggy Hill, held by the Gurkhas, were relieved every three or five days since it was only 15 yards from Japanese positions and being under constant attack, no sleep was possible. One of the most dashing attacks of the campaign took place when Gibraltar Hill, held by Rajputana Rifles, was taken by the enemy in a night attack. The Rajputana Rifles counter-attacked but, already weak, failed to take the pinnacle. The 3/10th Bn. in reserve, were finally called in, commanded by Lt.-Col. F.R. Cosens, who was later awarded the D.S.O. and O.B.E. Drawing their kukris they charged up the slopes, in some places almost sheer. The enemy had placed his flag on the top, but it was soon wrenched down. 125 Jap bodies were found afterwards. Jem. Bhakat Bahadur Rai who led the attack was awarded the M.C. ; 158 Field Regiment supported the attack.

In addition, the Division spared, for several days, 4th M.L.I. to assist 2nd Division by a battalion attack; a detachment of 6 Mahratta was sent to help 17th Division at Bishenpur. On June 22nd, the main road between Kohima and Imphal was reopened. The Division, ready now to move, were anxious to storm forward on the heels of the beaten enemy and to capture Tamu, but supplies were not available and the attack was delayed for a month.

Meanwhile, after their unsuccessful frontal attacks, the enemy began to infiltrate into the plain behind Shenam position. One night a party reached Palel aerodrome and blew up 2 Spitfires. A series of attacks were, however, under way by 4 and 6 Mahratta Light Infantry and the 2/19 Hyderabad Regiment (now the 2 Kumaon). The 2nd Indian Anti-Tank Regt. also helped, operating as infantry. Here, Hav. Surat Singh won the I.D.S.M., fighting as an infantryman ; 4 M.M.'s and 15 "Mentions" were awarded to the Regiment. The enemy were cleared from their positions on Langgol Hill.

*   *   *

"Fighting Cock" Attack on Tamu

DURING THE FIVE DAYS previous to the attack on Tamu on July 24th no less than 120 guns were concentrated to support the attack. The gunners, under Brigadier R.W. Andrews, D.S.O., M.C., the C. R. A., showed the enemy their quality.

One target would be shot up for 15 minutes, another for two minutes; everything was done to keep the enemy guessing and to shake his morale. Two veteran artillery regiments with the Division, 158 Field and 3rd Indian Field Regts.—men of Madras, Hyderabad and the Punjab—were assisted by the artillery of 2nd Division and 33rd Corps.

With other reserves available all ten battalions of 23rd Division were free for the actual assault. 37 Brigade made the frontal attack, the main fighting falling to 3/10 G. R. in their assault on Scraggy Hill. In hand-to-hand fighting Jem. Kharkabahadur Rai of this battalion, was awarded an immediate I. O. M. Sapper Sarja Singh, R.I.E., was awarded the M. M. when, in support of 3/10 G. R., he blew in a Jap bunker.

1 Brigade, already being experienced in encircling, went round the right flank across some very bad country. 1st Patiala and 1st Bn. Seaforths put in an attack on the road.

49 Brigade, supplied from the air, carried out a circular movement to cut the Japanese retreat. 4th Mahrattas were sent under Major Mackay, D S.O., M.C.

to cut the road. A road block was erected when Japs counter-attacked from Battle Hill and Bulldozer Corner and drove them back. By now the Battalions were very much weaker than before—companies were only 50 to 60 men strong, and a battalion had about 400 men.

These counter-attacks had been made by two fresh Japanese battalions sent to make a last effort to stop the attack and although eventually driven from their commanding positions by 6 M. L. I. and 5 Rajputana Rifles, the delay caused allowed a full regiment and supporting arms of the enemy to escape. The main assault was a complete success and the operation finished quicker than expected.

1 Brigade linked with 49 Brigade actually on Lokchao Bridge, the 1st Patialas meeting the 6 M. L. I. After this had been accomplished 5 Brigade of 2nd Division moved

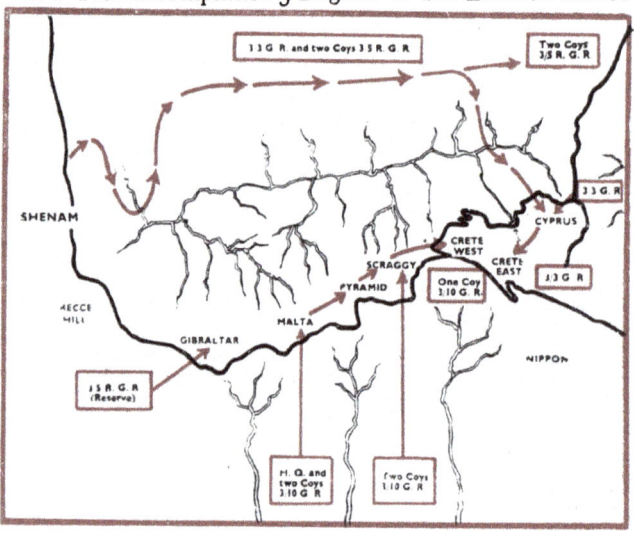

37 BRIGADE ON 24TH JULY 1944. After the relief of 20th Division 23rd Division was on the Shenam position. This shows 37 Brigades' attack when 23rd Division assaulted down the road to Tamu.

forward to occupy Tamu. It was then that the troops were able to realize what their attacks had meant to the enemy. Tamu, scene of desolation, was filled with Japanese dead and dying. Hundreds were wounded or suffering from hunger and disease.

The Burma chapter of 23rd Division was drawing to a close and, after $2\frac{1}{2}$ years fighting, they were relieved by 11 (EA) Division.

On August 18th the East Africans left Tamu and 11th (Kenya) Bn. K. A. R. fought their first action, attacking "Jambo Hill". 23rd Division had handed over.

The job 23rd Division had helped 14th Army to complete was summed up by General Slim—the task given to the Army had been fulfilled. The defences of Northern India had been secured. Five Japanese Divisions, 15th, 18th, 31st, 33rd and 55th had been destroyed as effective fighting formations, others had suffered considerably. Approximately, 50,000 Japanese had been killed. Most of the tanks and vehicles the enemy had brought into Assam had been lost, over 250 guns had been captured. Only 600 enemy had been made prisoner, an effective indication of the quality of the Japanese soldier.

Notable contributions by the "Fighting Cock" Division to these figures were more than 2,800 counted killed—at least 2,400 during the Imphal battle. They had taken more prisoners than any other Division—120. In terms of ground captured an area of Burma, more than twice the size of Ireland, had been liberated.

PHOTOGRAPHS OVERLEAF

This series was taken by cameramen who went forward with the fighting troops, and depicts the familiar scenes of some of the fiercest battles that took place—Scraggy and the neighbouring features; the Tamu road area ; the Lokchao River.

The mud and mist of the Burma monsoon is apparent, and illustrates some of the natural conditions under which the troops fought, and the difficulties encountered whilst defeating the Japanese.

On the steep side of LINCH HILL. L/Nk. Dambar Bahadur Sunwar seen outside an abandoned Jap position. Men lived for days on end in holes such as these.

The road which leads to TAMU with the hill CRETE WEST top left. A Sepoy, with back to camera, lights a cigarette.

A view from SCRAGGY to MALTA HILL, from where Scraggy used to be attacked. A scene of savage fighting. In foreground, a heap of Japanese helmets and equipment.

ON SCRAGGY. *The smell of death lingers over the place. Men of 3/10 G.R. clear away litter; bodies were found beneath caved-in Jap bunkers.*

Men of 3/10 G.R. just after the glorious victory of Scraggy which is discernible in the background mist.

O.N SCRAGGY soon after the victory ; Lt. P. P. Dunkley, M. C., inspects Jap gelignite bombs used against him and his men during the battle.

The winding road which leads to NIPPON PEAK and beyond to TAMU. In foreground, Hav. Dhan Singh Thapa and Rfn. Lal Bahadur Rai.

Another view of the road which leads to TAMU, taken from Scraggy. On extreme right, shrouded in mist, is NIPPON PEAK.

A VIEW of the PALEL-TAMU ROAD, seen under conditions of monsoon mud and mist.

On the TAMU ROAD under monsoon conditions, Bengal Sappers and Miners clear away mud and effect repairs.

PALEL—TAMU ROAD. Bengal Sappers and Miners doing maintenance work on roadway to keep it open for traffic.

Due to an extremely severe monsoon, the biggest landslide during the Imphal fighting occurred on the Palel-Tamu road about 20 miles N.W. of Tamu.

Supply of food and ammunition was maintained under great difficulty by the R.I.A.S.C.

LOKCHAO RIVER. Soldier passes across a rope bridge over the river in spate. The bridge led from a side track 4 miles North of Tamu Road.

Bridge over the LOKCHAO RIVER constructed by Indian Engineers. The original bridge was blown up by retreating Japs.

Another view of the LOKCHAO RIVER. Boat crosses about 3/4 miles east of TAMU.

Training for "Zipper"

SENT INTO ALF SEA reserve the Division went first to Shillong in Eastern India and from there on leave.

By October, 1944, refreshed Battalions were at strength again, and the Division moved over 2,000 miles across India to Nasik, north of Bombay. From that time until late August, 1945, when they embarked for Malaya, combined operations training was carried out. The three brigades were at Bombay, Nasik and Poona, alternately changing with each other. Maj.-Gen. O. L. Roberts left the Division to command 34 Corps as a Lieutenant-General, after his fine leadership in the campaign, and Maj.-General D. C. Hawthorn, came from 15 Corps to take command.

Why the Salt?

WHEN THE DIVISION arrived on the coast, it was the first time many sepoys had seen the sea. One platoon asked their commander *"Where does it all come from?"* and then followed it with *"Where does it all go to?"*. Answers, unfortunately, were not recorded!

Training was carried out constantly. The men spent hours practising, embarking and disembarking on the beaches from landing craft. Drivers waterproofed their vehicles and then drove them through the surf to get confidence in the proofing. Commanders, from the Lance Naik with his Bren Group, to the General, practised their job and got to know their new men.

When the monsoon broke, the ground became deep in mud. Temperatures of over a hundred degrees made battle schemes—"Princess" and "Countess", to give the code names for only two—not easy in a full pack.

But the Division, living in tents, kept fit, the malaria figure low. Security was good, although there were many rumours. One officer who joined the Division was seriously assured that Northern China was to be the objective of the next attack.

On VE-Day the Division was out on Exercise Cock 1. A special ration (liquor !) celebrated the first step to Victory. The training recommenced. By the beginning of August everyone knew their task and place in amphibious attack. Staff officers at Div. HQ knew that Malaya was the objective.

*   *   *   *

Attack on Malaya

"*THANK GOD, We're off, I wonder where we are going,*" were the thoughts of most men as they embarked on the ships at Bombay and Madras for operation "Zipper". The first troops embarked at Bombay on the 23rd August. Two days after sailing the men were told their destination. Classes in Malay, lectures from SEA Guides on the country and descriptions of the beaches they were to land on were given. Everyone received a pamphlet on, Malaya. All were prepared for fighting but few expected the Japanese to resist.

On 29th August, 49 Brigade left Bombay and on September 1st 37 Brigade embarked from Madras, main Division Headquarters travelling with them. After a pleasant, uninterrupted voyage, the convoy reached the Malacca Straits and the ships parted, 37 Brigade to carry out an assault landing at Sepang on D-Day,

9th September, while to the South at Port Dickson 1 and 49 Brigades had to land on D-3. Both landings were peacefully carried out.

The same day as they were put on the beach, 1 Brigade went inland and captured Seremban. On September 15th a parade was held there at which the Japanese Commander made ceremonial surrender to Maj.-Gen. D. C. Hawthorn. During September the Division was sent to different parts of Malaya. 37 Brigade and Div HQ to Seremban, 1 Brigade South to the coast at Malacca and 49 Brigade to Kuala Lipis on the East Coast. The job of restoring law to Malaya was started, looting and banditry being quickly suppressed. Force 136 kept giving information as to where the Japanese were concentrated.

Then swiftly new orders were issued—the Division was to move to Java where trouble was reported. Operation "Persil" on Sept. 22nd-23rd dealt with the move. No maps and little information about the Javanese could be found, so intelligence started a hunt for facts and figures about this little known territory. Q Branch faced with the job of moving the Division and its supplies were started into feverish activity. A C.R.A.'s Brigade was formed to provide a fourth Brigade. As reports arrived of further disturbances and riots, preparations were speeded up.

On 24th September Tac HQ flew to Batavia, followed by the main HQ who landed on October 3rd. They found the city quiet and the people friendly, cheering as they moved to their HQ which was started in the N.K.P.M. building. Shortly afterwards they were joined by 1 and 37 Brigades. However the quiet situation did not last for long. As captured Japanese arms got into the hands of the Indonesians, they saw their opportunity in lack of control to strike for independence. The most difficult job the Division had ever tackled was starting: the rescue of internees and restoration of law and order in Java.

*   *   *

ARREST OF JAPANESE GENERALS for allowing weapons to be handed over to unauthorised persons. Maj. Gen. Yamamoto hands sword to Maj. Gen. Hawthorn.

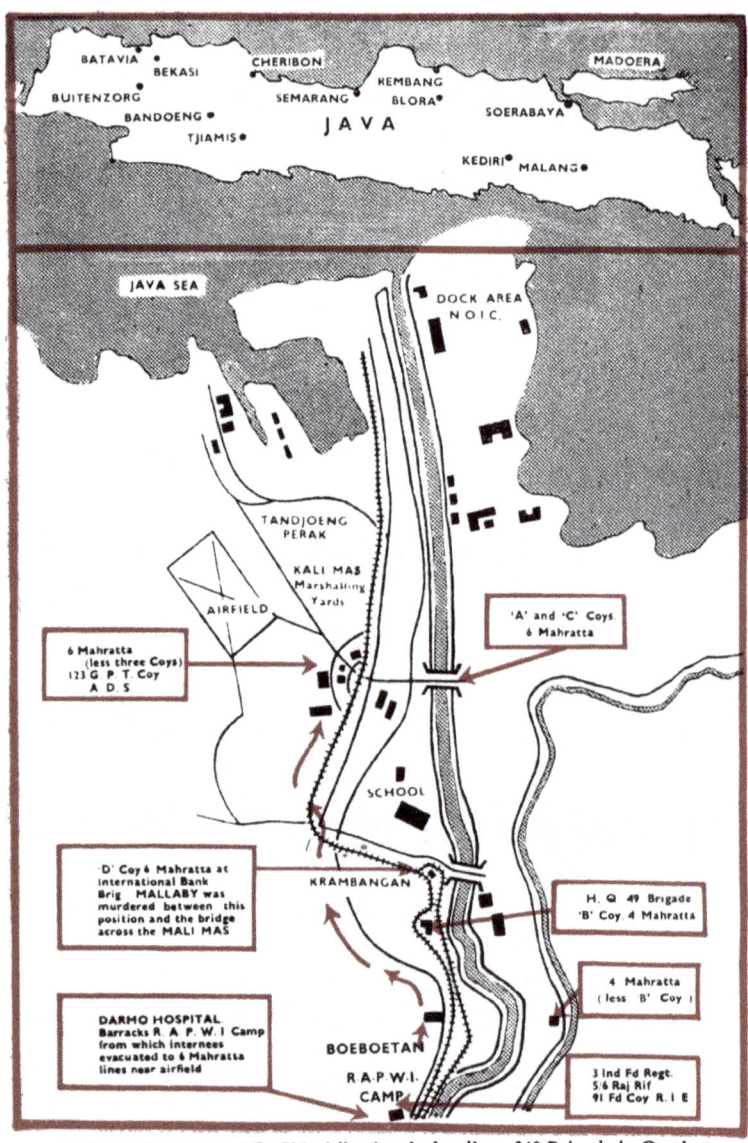

JAVA AND SOERABAYA, following the landing of 49 Brigade in October, 1945. Scene of Brig. Mallaby's murder, and steps taken by the Brigade to rescue internees.

49 Brigade in Soerabaya

ON OCTOBER 24TH, after a six days voyage, 49 Brigade, commanded by Brigadier A.W.S. Mallaby, C.I.E., O.B.E., arrived at Soerabaya on the north coast of Java. A deputation from the Indonesians was received at Brigade HQ by Col. L.H.O. Pugh, D.S.O., second-in-command of the Brigade. Straightaway he explained the tasks that the British forces had come to do—to safeguard and evacuate the internees who had suffered under the Japanese for $3\frac{1}{2}$ years, disarm and remove the Japanese and, in Soerabaya, to cooperate with the Indonesian Republican Government so far as was necessary to carry out these tasks.

From the outset the Indonesians in the area were suspicious of the Brigade's motives, partly due to the earlier arrival of a Dutch Naval officer. But the first meetings were, on the surface, cordial. From 10 o'clock on the 27th, however, the situation deteriorated rapidly and in the afternoon of that day the Indonesians left secretly and the extremists' preparation for war became obvious.

Broadcasts started and the civilian population was warned by the Indonesians that they were about to attack the British. At 4.30, October 28th, the uniformed T.R.I. treacherously attacked all Brigade positions. In the late afternoon of 31st October, Brig. Mallaby went out with three staff officers and some Indonesian leaders on a tour of the town to try and stop the shooting. The worst trouble was at the International Bank where several hundred armed Indonesians, who had kept the building under fire for two days; were being whipped into a frenzy by mob leaders. The moderate leaders lost all control. Firing broke out. After two hours some of the mob approached and the Brigadier asked them to take him to a party leader for they had come to stop the fighting. Then without any warning one fired a revolver at the Brigadier who shortly afterwards died. Two of the officers with him escaped, after being wounded, and took the news to HQ.

The situation was dangerous. Ammunition was running short in the Brigade. Food was rationed. Plans were made for a breakout to the coast from the positions in the centre of the town which were being constantly attacked by massed Indonesians. Many platoons, in one case a company, had been overrun. The fighting died down during the night but flared up again the next morning. However after further negotiations the Indonesians agreed to allow the Brigade to concentrate in the port area and again they started to try to carry out their tasks.

At this time the R.I.A.S.C. with the Brigade were feeding 65,000 RAPWI from Japanese supplies. The first convoy to evacuate internees ran at this time with 27 3-tonners under command of Subedar Tek Chand who won the M.C. When the convoy was attacked he and his I.O.R.s in defence of their vehicles carrying women and children, wrote one of the finest pages in the history of the Indian Sepoy. They fought to the last to protect their charges, eleven were killed, twenty-six believed killed out of forty who started. They saved ninety internees out of some eight hundred in the convoy. 49 Brigade had now come under command of 5th Division.

The situation throughout Java was confused. Two big RAPWI camps near Semarang, at Magelang and Ambarawa, were looked after by the 3/10 Gurkhas now in the CRA's Brigade. This Brigade was made up of the 2 Ind. Anti-Tank, 2/19 Hyderabad, and 11 Cavalry. For more than two weeks, the Gurkhas were supplied entirely by Royal Air Force. It was at Semarang that Hav. Dalip Singh M. M. of 91 Ind. Fd. Coy. R. I. E. was awarded a bar to his Medal, when after being wounded in the stomach, he went on clearing mines.

37 Brigade moved to Bandoeng, where the biggest RAPWI camp in Java was situated. The 65,000 internees were being murdered at 100 a day, when 3/5 R. G. R. reached the town on 17th October. Later a convoy of 200 vehicles running supplies to them was ambushed three times. Twenty-four were killde, including three drivers of the four ambulances in the convoy. There were several M. Cs. awarded for gallantry on this run, including one for Capt. L. Thompson, RIASC, the M. T. Commander.

By January the situation nearer Batavia was more peaceful and it was decided to move the main part of the Division to Bandoeng. When they arrived on 16th Feb. the town was split into two by the railway, south of which was held by the Indonesians, the north being commanded by 37 Brigade. It bore all the appearances of a front line ; machine gun positions, sandbag barricades and mortar positions facing each other. In March an operation to ensure the water supply of the town was carried out by 49 Brigade, assisted by 36 Brigade. This was speeded up by Indonesians from over the railway line, but the T. R. I. had evacuated finally when the Brigade advanced. After this job 37 changed with 1 Brigade who had guarded the Buitenzorg area. A full scale operation was necessary to open the road. 49 Brigade in the meantime had occupied Tjiater, North of Bandoeng.

By June the task had been finished in Bandoeng and the Dutch forces took over. The Division returned to Batavia ; due to their efforts many tens of thousands of internees had been rescued from great danger. The price paid in Java in killed, wounded and missing was 1,348 men from all ranks.

In the last four years the men of the " Fighting Cock " Division have worthily maintained and added to the glorious traditions of the Indian Army.

Pipe Band of 1st Bn. SEAFORTH HIGHLANDERS provided music during King's Birthday Parade held on Batavia Racecourse, June '46.

SOERABAYA FIGHTING

By Havildar Clerk S. N. Nath, 123 Coy. R.I.A.S.C.

ON 28TH OCTOBER '45 at about 1500 hours our detachment landed at Soerabaya Dock, Java. As we passed through the streets with our vehicles there were absolutely no signs of any suspicious activities amongst the Indonesians in the city. Everything seemed to be peaceful and as usual. We were allotted some Dutch bungalows on the outskirts of the city near the Dock Kalimas.

It was at about 1800 hours and we were all very busy fixing ourselves up after 4 days at sea, when we heard rifle and machine gun shots from the direction of the city. Capt. H. McGregor, who was O.C. of the detachment at Soerabaya, was with us and ordered us to take defence positions. We were all on guard throughout the night. Nothing unpleasant happened that night.

On the following day, at about 0700 hours when we were all taking tea, a sentry came and reported that armed Indonesians were gathering in the bungalows on the other side of the street. We at once occupied our defence positions and started firing when we saw that the Indonesians were charging us. At that time we were about 120 men strong. But the Indonesians were 4 or 5 times our number. Heavy firing from rifles and machine guns took place on both sides, and we inflicted heavy casualties on the Indonesians. But the Indonesians still attempted to enter our lines with stubborn determination. To our utmost alarm our ammunition stock was rapidly diminishing. In this precarious situation, we called for help from the 6/5 Mahratta L. I. Headquarters about 5 furlongs from our lines. They came and fired their mortars at the Indonesians and in the meantime ordered us to retreat with our vehicles. Under cover of the mortar fire we withdrew and drove our vehicles to a place where the Indonesians had built positions and were well on guard. No sooner did we reach there than the Indonesians surrounded us and started firing on all sides. We at once got down from our vehicles and took up positions in the drain on both sides of the road, and retaliated with rifle fire until our ammunition was exhausted. We were awaiting further events, when we received orders from our commander to save our lives. I was by that time dead tired due to thirst and burning sun. With the greatest difficulty, I dragged myself out of the drain into the bushes by the road, and began creeping through the long grass for the rest of the day. Shots rom the Indonesians' rifles and machine guns were passing over my head making a hissing sound. I was expecting an Indonesian bullet from a rifle or machine gun to pierce my brain. But luckily for me, that did not happen. I continued to make slow but steady progress, creeping through the bushes without interruption, though it was in no way a happy experience. At one time I happened to come very near to an Indonesian who, under cover of the long grass was firing in the direction from which we had withdrawn. I at once realised that our positions were somewhere in that direction. This gave me some hope, and I stole away quietly from that place, crossed a nullah, and, continuing to crawl, reached the end of that long grassy field. I noticed some bungalows a short distance away, and peered through the long grass to discover who the inmates were. To my great relief, I found that they were men of our platoon.

This was the end of my adventures in Soerabaya. On the following day we discovered that 10 men were missing in the action. Later on they were found killed in that very drain from which I slipped away.

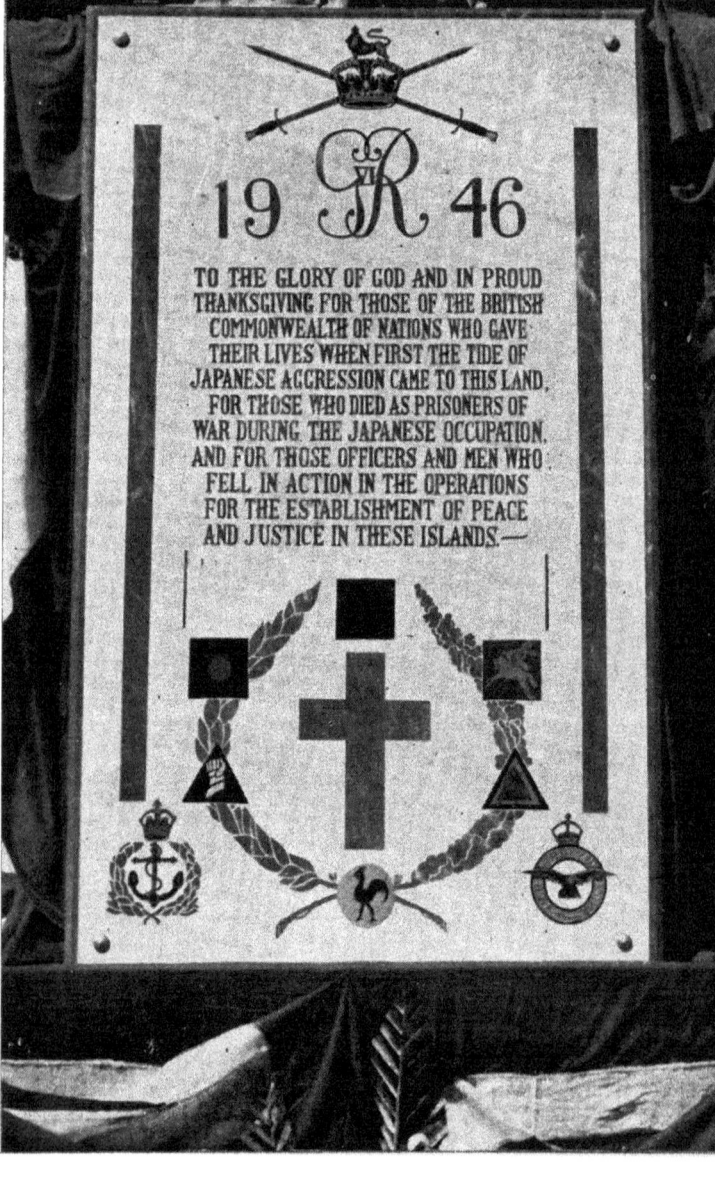

23rd INDIAN DIVISION AS IN AUGUST 1945
Formations/Units and Commanders

Div. Comd.	.. Major General	D. C. HAWTHORN, C.B., D.S.O
C. R. A.	.. Brigadier	.. R. B. W. BETHELL, D. S. O.
C. R. E.	.. Lt. Col.	.. R. E. HOLLOWAY, M.B.E.
Comd. 1 Bde	.. Brigadier	.. R. C. M. KING, D.S.O., O B.E.
CO 1 SEAFORTH	.. Lt. Col.	.. E. H. B. NEILL
CO 1/16 PUNJAB	.. Lt. Col.	.. J. A. V. BOLAM
CO 1 PATIALA	.. Lt. Col.	.. BIKRAMDEV SINGH GILL
Comd. 37 Bde	.. Brigadier	.. N. MACDONALD, D.S O.
CO 3/3 R. G. R.	.. Lt. Col.	.. A. R. C. K. GREENWAY
CO 3/5 R. G. R.	.. Lt. Col.	.. G. P. V. SANDERS, D.S.O.
CO 3/10 G. R.	.. Lt. Col.	.. H. G. EDWARDES
Comd. 49 Bde	.. Brigadier	.. A W. S. MALLABY, C. I.E., O.B.E.
CO 4 MAHRATTA	.. Lt. Col.	.. P. N. W. DOYLE, M.C.
CO 6 MAHRATTA	.. Lt. Col.	.. A. K. CROOKSHANK
CO 5 RAJ RIF	.. Lt. Col.	.. N. M. BRODIE
OC 5/8 PUNJAB (Recce Bn)	.. Lt. Col.	.. R. S. STEED
OC 6/8 PUNJAB (M.G. Bn)	.. Lt. Col.	.. C. H. GENDERS
OC 2 HYBAD (Div. Def. Bn)	.. Lt. Col.	.. F. D. ROBERTSON, M.C.
178 FIELD REGT.	.. Lt. Col.	.. H. J. HAMILTON, R.A.
CO 2 IND FIELD REGT.	.. Lt. Col.	.. J. F. S. RENDALL, D.S.O., R.A.
CO 28 IND MTN REGT.	.. Lt. Col.	.. H. LANDON, O.B.E., R.A.
CO 2 IND A TK REGT.	.. Lt. Col.	.. D. R. CORNER, R A.

INDIAN DIVISIONS WON A FINE REPUTATION IN WORLD WAR TWO

Field Marshal Auchinleck, Commander-in-Chief of the British Indian Army from 1942, asserted that the British "*couldn't have come through both wars (World War I and II) if they hadn't had the British Indian Army*". British Prime Minister Winston Churchill also paid tribute to "*the unsurpassed bravery of Indian soldiers and officers*".

Between 1945 and 1947, the Director of Public Relations, War Department, Government of India, published a series of short publications covering the individual histories of the WWII Indian Divisions. They followed a consistent format, having between 44 and 48 pages within illustrated soft card covers. They have an average of 50 monochrome photographic illustrations, and each has a full colour centrespread depicting a scene from the Division's wartime operations (drawn by official war artists). They were printed at various presses in Bombay and New Delhi, and each contains at least one map.

As condensed histories they are useful – particularly those which relate to Divisions for which no other record was ever produced.

The British Indian Army during World War II began the war, in 1939, numbering just under 200,000 men. By the end of the war, it had become the largest volunteer army in history, rising to over 2.5 million men in August 1945. Serving in divisions of infantry, armour and a fledgling airborne force, they fought on three continents: in Africa, Europe and Asia.

This Army fought in Ethiopia against the Italian Army, in Egypt, Libya, Tunisia and Algeria against both the Italian and German Army and, after the Italian surrender, against the German Army in Italy. However, the bulk of the British Indian Army was committed to fighting the Japanese Army, first during the British defeats in Malaya and the retreat from Burma to the Indian border; later, after resting and refitting for the victorious advance back into Burma, as part of the largest British Empire army ever formed. These campaigns cost the lives of over 87,000 Indian service- men, while another 34,354 were wounded, and 67,340 became prisoners of war. Their valour was recognised with the award of some 4,000 decorations, and 18 members of the British Indian Army were awarded the Victoria Cross or the George Cross.

RED EAGLES
The Story of the 4th Indian Division
9781474537520

During the Second World War, the 4th Indian Division was in the vanguard of nine campaigns in the Mediterranean theatre, Egypt, Eritrea, Syria, Tunisia, Italy and Greece. The 4th Division captured 150,000 prisoners and suffered 25,000 casualties, more than the strength of a whole division. It won over 1,000 honours and awards, which included four Victoria Crosses and three George Crosses. Field Marshal Lord Wavell wrote: "The fame of this Division will surely go down as one of the greatest fighting formations in military history."

THE FIGHTING FIFTH
History of the 5th Indian Division
9781474537513

As described in much greater detail in Anthony Brett James's book 'The Ball of Fire', the division saw active service in East Africa, North Africa and Burma.

GOLDEN ARROW
The Story of the 7th Indian Division
9781474537506

The role of this division is also duplicated by a much larger work: the book by Brig. M. R. Roberts. However, this booklet gives a good account of Kohima and Imphal and the crossing of the Irrawaddy. In 1945, the division was flown into Siam, so becoming the first Allied formation to re-enter South East Asia.

ONE MORE RIVER
The Story of the 8th Indian Division
Biferno, Trigno, Sangro, Moro, Rapido, Arno, Senio, Santerno, Po, Adige

9781474537490

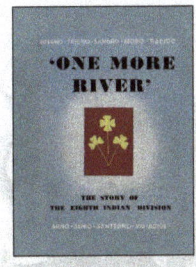

The 8th Indian Division started its overseas service in the Middle East in the garrisoning of Iraq and then the invasion of Persia to secure the oil fields of the area for the Allies, before moving to Italy in 1943. Landing at Taranto, it pushed up the length of the peninsula in a series of major battles: breaking the Sangro Line, forcing the Rapido and turning the defences at Cassino, breaking the stubborn German resistance at Monte Grande and, finally, forcing the Po River. It won four VCs, 26 DSOs and 149 MCs along the way. During the war the 8th Indian Division sustained casualties totalling 2,012 dead, 8,189 wounded and 749 missing.

BLACK CAT DIVISION
17th Indian Division

9781474537483

This formation was committed to Burma from the early days when the British were in full flight from the invading Japanese. It remained in Burma right through to the end, when the starving remnants of the Japanese Army were making their own desperate retreat.

TIGER HEAD
The Story of the 26th Indian Division
Arakan, Ragoon

9781474537452

This is a history of the division said later by the Japanese to have been the opponent which they most feared. The 26th held the Allied monsoon line in the Arakan during two such seasons, repulsing every attack launched against it. Later it made a series of leap-frog landings down the coast to clinch the issue in the Arakan. It was the first division to enter Ragoon, invading the city from the sea.

A HAPPY FAMILY
The Story of the Twentieth Indian Division, April 1942-August 1945

9781474537476

One of the few Indian divisions in the 14th Army trained specifically for the war in Burma. Raised in Bangalore in 1942, it commenced active operations in late 1943 and served from Imphal through to the end. It established the 14th Army's first brigade-head across the Chindwin and its second such brigade-head across the Irrawaddy. Its final task was to round up the Japanese in French Indochina.

THE TWENTY THIRD INDIAN DIVISION
"The Fighting Cock Division"
Burma, Malaya, Java

9781474537469

The Fighting Cock Division is well recorded in the book by Doulton. This book gives coverage of the heavy fighting at the Kohima Battle, the capture of Tamu, the reoccupation of Malaya in August 1945, and then its strange role on the island of Java – concurrently disarming the Japanese garrison, fighting the insurgent Indonesian nationalists, and caring for 65,000 former internees pending the arrival of a new Dutch administration.

TEHERAN TO TRIESTE
The Story Of The Tenth Indian Division

9781783317028

This History deals with the 10th Indian Div's exploits in Iraq (under Maj Gen "Bill" Slim) its role in the Libyan battles leading up to El Alamein, the following two years of garrison duties in Cyprus and Syria, and finally, its fighting services in the Italian campaign (from Ortona onwards).

THE STORY OF THE 25th INDIAN DIVSION
The Arakan Campaign
9781783317585

Formed in Southern India in August 1942 for defence of that area in case of Japanese invasion, the "Ace of Spades" Division had its baptism of fire in Arakan in February 1944. It served throughout the remainder of that campaign the climax being the battle of Tamandu. Its victorious fight for the Kangaw roadblock was considered by many to have been the fiercest battle of the entire Burma war, while its liberation of Akyab was the first convincing proof to the rest of the world that the tide had turned against the Japanese.

DAGGER DIVISION
The Story Of The 19th Indian Division
9781783317035

Raised in the late 1941, the 19th was the first "standard" Indian Division. Its troops were the first to breach the Japanese defence line in Burma and to raise the flag at Fort Dufferin. It crossed the Chindwin in November 1944, driving on to Mandalay and Ragoon during seven months of continuous fighting. The 19th's exploits are graphically described also in John Masters' personal memoir, *The Road Past Mandalay*.

www.ingramcontent.com/pod-product-compliance
Lightning Source LLC
Chambersburg PA
CBHW041928090426
42743CB00021B/3472